History of America

THE RECONSTRUCTION ERA

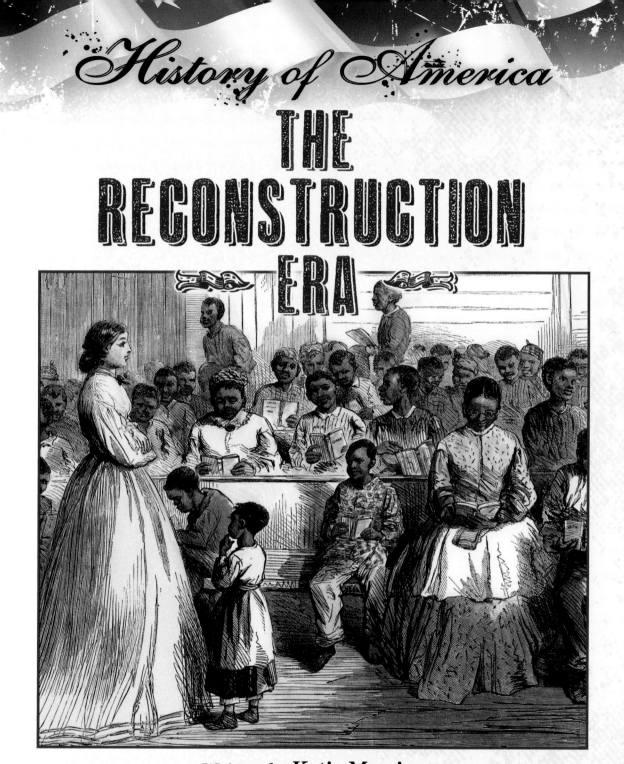

Written by **Katie Marsico**

rourkeeducationalmedia.com

www.rourkeeducationalmedia.com

Photo credits: North Wind Picture Archives, cover, 16, 22, 30, 40; iStockphoto, cover, 5, 11, 19, 27, 35; Library of Congress, 4, 7 (left), 7 (right), 15, 23, 29, 34, 37 (left), 37 (right), 39, 42 (top), 42 (middle), 42 (bottom), 43 (top), 43 (middle), 43 (bottom), 45 (left); North Wind Picture Archives/Photolibrary, 6, 9, 10, 13, 14, 18, 21, 25, 26, 28, 33, 44, 45 (right)

Edited by Jill Sherman

Cover design by Nicola Stratford, bdpublishing.com

Interior Layout by Pam McCollum

Library of Congress PCN Data

Marsico, Katie
The Reconstruction Era / Katie Marsico.
 ISBN 978-1-62169-828-9 (hard cover)
 ISBN 978-1-62169-723-7 (soft cover)
 ISBN 978-1-62169-932-3 (e-Book)
Library of Congress Control Number: 2013936296

Also Available as:

ROURKE'S
e-Books

Rourke Educational Media
Printed in the United States of America,
North Mankato, Minnesota

rourkeeducationalmedia.com

customerservice@rourkeeducationalmedia.com • PO Box 643328 Vero Beach, Florida 32964

TABLE OF CONTENTS

ABRAHAM LINCOLN

and his

Emancipation Proclamation

Whereas On the Twenty-second day of September, in the year of our Lord one thousand eight hundred and sixty-two, a Proclamation was issued by the President of the United States, containing among other things the following, to-wit:

"That on the first day of January, in the year of our Lord one thousand eight hundred and sixty-three, all persons held as slaves within any State, or designated part of a State, the people whereof shall then be in rebellion against the United States, shall be then, thenceforward and forever free, and the executive government of the United States, including the military and naval authority thereof, will recognize and maintain the freedom of such persons, and will do no act or acts to repress such persons, or any of them, in any efforts they may make for their actual freedom.

"That the executive will, on the first day of January aforesaid, by proclamation, designate the States and parts of States, if any, in which the people thereof respectively shall then be in rebellion against the United States, and the fact that any State, or the people thereof, shall on that day be in good faith represented in the Congress of the United States by members chosen thereto at elections wherein a majority of the qualified voters of such State shall have participated, shall, in the absence of strong countervailing testimony, be deemed conclusive evidence that such State and the people thereof are not then in rebellion against the United States."

Now, therefore, I, ABRAHAM LINCOLN, President of the United States, by virtue of the power in me vested as Commander-in-Chief of the Army and Navy of the United States in time of actual armed rebellion against the authority and government of the United States, and as a fit and necessary war measure for suppressing said rebellion, do, on this first day of January, in the year of our Lord one thousand eight hundred and sixty-three, and in accordance with my purpose so to do, publicly proclaim for the full period of one hundred days from the day the first above mentioned order, and designate as the States and parts of States wherein the people thereof respectively are this day in rebellion against the United States, the following, to-wit:

ARKANSAS, TEXAS, LOUISIANA (except the parishes of St. Bernard, Plaquemines, Jefferson, St. John, St. Charles, St. James, Ascension, Assumption, Terre Bonne, Lafourche, St. Mary, St. Martin, and Orleans, including the city of New Orleans), MISSISSIPPI, ALABAMA, FLORIDA, GEORGIA, SOUTH CAROLINA, NORTH CAROLINA and VIRGINIA (except the forty-eight counties designated as West Virginia, and also the counties of Berkley, Accomac, Northampton, Elizabeth City, York, Princess Ann and Norfolk, including the cities of Norfolk and Portsmouth), and which excepted parts are, for the present, left precisely as if this Proclamation were not issued.

And by virtue of the power and for the purpose aforesaid, I do order and declare that all persons held as slaves within said designated States and parts of States are and henceforward shall be free; and that the executive government of the United States, including the military and naval authorities thereof, will recognize and maintain the freedom of said persons.

And I hereby enjoin upon the people so declared to be free, to abstain from all violence, unless in necessary self-defence, and I recommend to them that in all cases, when allowed, they labor faithfully for reasonable wages.

And I further declare and make known that such persons of suitable condition, will be received into the armed service of the United States to garrison forts, positions, stations and other places, and to man vessels of all sorts in said service.

And upon this act, sincerely believed to be an act of justice, warranted by the Constitution, upon military necessity, I invoke the considerate judgment of mankind, and the gracious favor of Almighty God.

In testimony whereof, I have hereunto set my name, and caused the seal of the United States to be affixed.

Done at the City of Washington, this first day of January, in the year of our Lord one thousand eight hundred

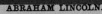

the President: ABRAHAM LINCOLN.

WILLIAM H. SEWARD, Secretary of State.

NOTE.---The rest of the slaves were afterwards freed by Legislation and Constitutional Amendments.

Chapter 1
THE DEATH OF A PRESIDENT

It was early morning on April 15, 1865. Americans nervously wondered what would happen to the United States now that President Abraham Lincoln was dead. The night before, John Wilkes Booth shot Lincoln during a play in Washington, D.C. The Civil War had ended only days before.

The North, called the **Union**, fought the South, called the **Confederacy**, from 1861 to 1865. After Lincoln was elected president in 1860, several southern states **seceded** from the Union. They decided to become their own country. These states were in favor of slavery, while Lincoln wanted to limit slavery. They feared that Lincoln would not allow them to own slaves.

Lincoln ordered war to force the southern states to come back to the Union. During the war, in January 1863, he issued his **Emancipation Proclamation**.

This document promised to free the slaves in the Confederacy, which made the South fight even harder. They knew their loss would mean the end of slavery.

John Wilkes Booth, a famous American stage actor, assassinated President Abraham Lincoln at Ford's Theatre, in Washington, D.C., on April 14, 1865.

On April 15, 1865 the country was at peace, but it faced many problems. Southern cities were destroyed. The states that seceded had to rejoin the United States. Northerners did not agree on how this should be done. Many people wanted the South to be punished for starting the long and expensive war. Finally, the end of the war freed millions of slaves in the South, as Lincoln had promised. Everyone wondered what roles and rights these men and women would have.

SURRENDER

The Civil War ended less than a week before Lincoln was murdered. On April 9, 1865 General Robert E. Lee surrendered his Confederate forces to Union commander Ulysses S. Grant at Appomattox Courthouse in central Virginia. Though several small battles occurred in the following weeks, Lee controlled most of the Confederate troops. His surrender in early April ended the major fighting.

The new role of former slaves in America was a question that troubled both southerners and northerners, blacks and whites, everyone from politicians to farmers. When President Lincoln died on April 15, 1865 the questions still had no answers. The country wondered how Vice President Andrew Johnson would address the nation's countless problems when he became president.

The Civil War ended when General Robert E. Lee surrendered to General Ulysses S. Grant at Appomattox Courthouse.

Abraham Lincoln led the United States through its greatest constitutional, military, and moral crisis, the American Civil War, preserving the Union and abolishing slavery.

"They seemed not to know... what was to be their fate since their great benefactor was dead, and their hopeless grief affected me more than almost anything else, though strong and brave men wept when I met them."

—U.S. Secretary of the Navy Gideon Welles describing a group of former slaves mourning Lincoln's death

All of these issues were the focus of Reconstruction, the period from 1863 to 1877. During this time politicians and citizens tried to rebuild the country. This would not be quick, or easy. Some groups were in favor of showing mercy to the South. They wanted to allow southern states to reenter the Union without harsh punishment. However, other northerners wanted to punish the South. They blamed these states for the hundreds of thousands of soldiers who died and the chaos that followed the bloodshed.

Politicians also debated the fate of former slaves and free blacks. The freed slaves hoped for liberty and the chance for equality and success. The politicians disagreed about how much the U.S. government should help the freed slaves. They argued over whether blacks should be allowed to vote in elections and attend school.

RECONSTRUCTION

Historians usually divide Reconstruction into three or four phases. The first phase was Presidential Reconstruction (1863–1867), when Reconstruction was controlled by the presidents. Historians sometimes divide this into two parts: Lincoln's Reconstruction and Johnson's Reconstruction. The next phase was Congressional Reconstruction or Radical Reconstruction (1867–1869). This was the period when Congress pushed through its plan for Reconstruction. The final phase of Reconstruction was Redemption Reconstruction (1869–1877), when white southerners took control and started to undo the changes made by the Republicans.

When slavery finally ended in America, former slaves took measures to find new homes and jobs, and to find lost family members.

> "His death is a terrible loss to the country... perhaps an even greater loss to the South than to the North, for Mr. Lincoln's humanity and kindness of heart stood between them and the party of the North who urge measures of vengeance and severity."
>
> —Nineteenth-century author Sidney George Fisher commenting on Lincoln's death

Officials could not agree on these or other important topics. And after Lincoln's death, with their leader gone, everyone wondered if the United States would ever truly be united again.

Chapter 2
REBUILDING A COUNTRY

Even before the war ended, Lincoln began to think about how the country would be reunited. Lincoln did not want to punish the rebel states. He did not sympathize with the South, but his first priority was rebuilding the country.

In late 1863 he announced a Reconstruction plan that reflected his beliefs. He thought 10 percent of the white males in former Confederate states should have to pledge their loyalty to the U.S. government. They would promise never to rebel again and to obey U.S. laws about slavery. Then, the rebellious states should be able to rejoin the Union and elect new state governments.

Republican congressmen, in particular a group known as the Radical Republicans, thought the president should be tougher on disloyal states. In 1864 these congressmen came up with their own plan for reuniting the country.

The Republicans argued that 50 percent of the white males in former Confederate states should have to swear their loyalty. Lincoln **vetoed** this plan. The president and Congress debated the best strategies for Reconstruction until the end of the war and Lincoln's death.

The first reaction of freed slaves was that they wanted to gain new knowledge to make better lives for themselves and their families.

The punishment of southern states was not the only issue. Most slaves were promised their freedom with the Emancipation Proclamation and became free after the war. After the Thirteenth Amendment became law in December 1865, the rest of the slaves gained their freedom.

Millions of former slaves, known as **freedmen**, were overjoyed. Families whose members had been sold to different owners could reunite. Marriages, which were forbidden to slaves, were now made official. Strong family bonds became the cornerstone of emerging black communities and churches.

However, the freedmen also struggled to find their new place in society. Most did not own homes or land. Most were not educated and could not read or write. They needed to find jobs. In addition, many white southerners were not pleased about the end of slavery. They wanted to keep their power over the former slaves. Sometimes they used violence against blacks.

FORTY ACRES AND A MULE

Union General William Tecumseh Sherman marched through the South toward the end of the war. He was faced by tens of thousands of freedmen who had no homes or money. To help them, he granted several former slave families a mule and 40 acres (16 hectares) of land. This property had once belonged to Confederate farm owners along the Georgia coast. Sherman's orders went into effect starting on January 16, 1865. However, President Johnson overturned the order in the fall of 1865. He gave the land back to its original owners.

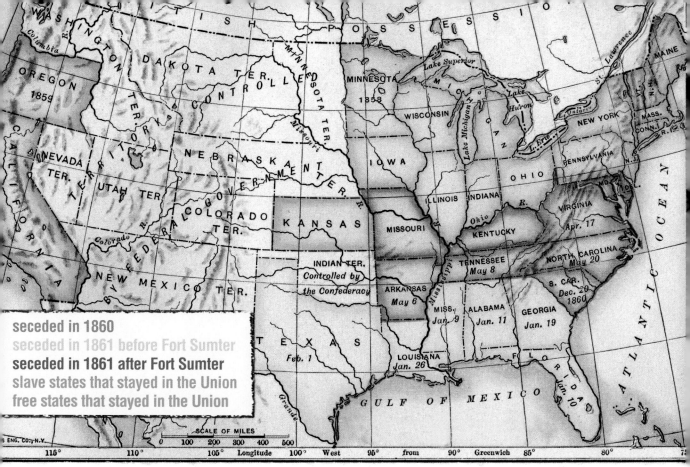

After the Civil War, the North and the South had to reunite.

The map legend reads:

seceded in 1860
seceded in 1861 before Fort Sumter
seceded in 1861 after Fort Sumter
slave states that stayed in the Union
free states that stayed in the Union

Congress formed the Freedmen's Bureau in March 1865. This organization was created to help the former slaves make the transition to freedom. It gave them food, clothing, and other everyday supplies. The Freedmen's Bureau offered aid to poor, white southerners as well. Its purpose was to help men and women in the South begin new lives after the war.

The U.S. Congress celebrates after passing the Thirteenth Amendment.

Everything changed when Johnson took office after Lincoln's murder. The new president blamed wealthy white southerners for the war. In his mind, there was no reason to punish the majority of white men and women who lived in the South. Most white southerners simply had to promise never to rebel again. They also promised to follow U.S. laws about slavery. Then they would be allowed to vote and hold government offices again. The very wealthy would have to personally ask Johnson for a pardon, which he almost always granted. Johnson also returned southern **plantations** to their original owners.

Andrew Johnson (1808–1875)

Andrew Johnson, the 17th President of the United States, became president at the time of Lincoln's assassination. His plans did not give protection to the former slaves, and he came into conflict with the Congress, culminating in his impeachment by the House of Representatives.

Rioters protesting the freeing of slaves burn a school for freedmen.

A WORLD FOR WHITE MEN ALONE

Congressmen hoped that President Johnson would help them improve life for the freedmen. It was soon clear that he did not want to grant former slaves equal rights. His beliefs became obvious when he said, "White men alone must manage the South."

Johnson was not interested in helping former slaves build new lives. He sided with poor white southerners, who feared that the freedmen would take their jobs. He believed that blacks and whites were not equal. He wanted whites to control the government in the South.

Johnson chose a temporary governor for each of the states that seceded. Each governor had to develop a new state constitution that outlawed secession and supported the Thirteenth Amendment.

> "I am very anxious about the future: and most about the principles which are to govern reconstruction: for as these principles are sound or unsound so will be the work & its results... The easiest & safest way seems to me to be... without regard to color... securing the right to vote to all citizens... This you know has long been my opinion. It is confirmed by observation more & more."
>
> —Antislavery politician Salmon P. Chase to Abraham Lincoln, April 11, 1865

By the end of 1865 all the former Confederate states followed the president's plan. Johnson announced that Reconstruction was complete and the country was reunited. The states prepared to send representatives to serve in Congress in Washington, D.C.

Unsurprisingly, Radical Republicans and other northern politicians did not agree with this plan. Slavery was ended, but nothing was done to protect the **civil rights** of freedmen.

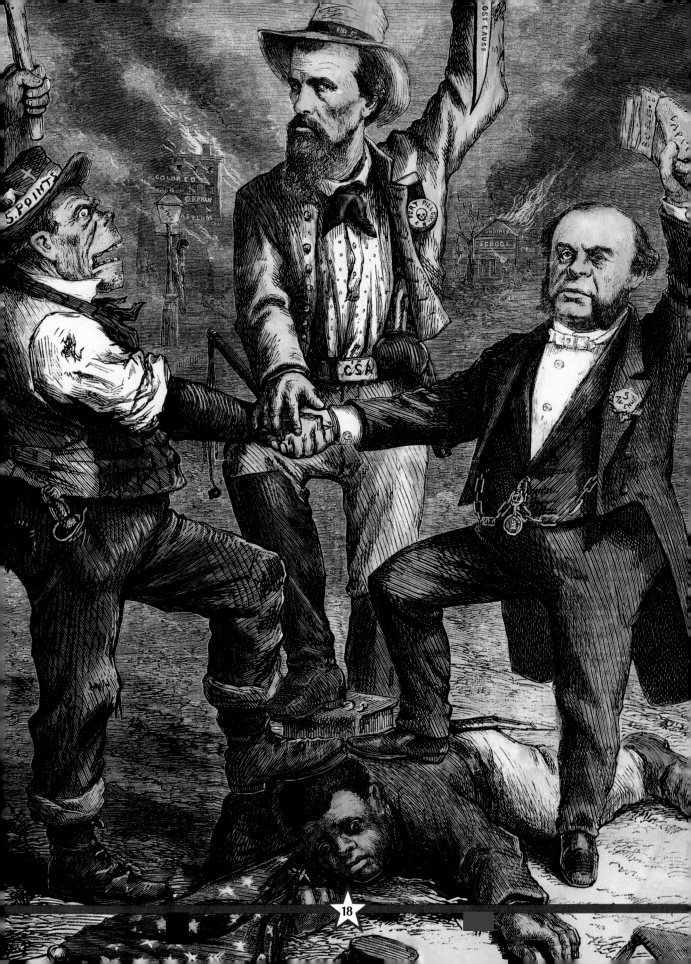

Chapter 3
A NEW PLAN FOR THE FUTURE

Newly elected southern senators and representatives arrived in Washington, D.C. in December 1865. They were not welcomed by the other politicians. Congress refused to seat them. Johnson was furious, but the Radical Republicans wanted to take a stand. They believed the president's plan had failed to rebuild the South.

Former Confederates had never sincerely apologized for the war against the United States. Even worse, many freedmen had little more freedom than slaves. Following the Civil War, several southern state governments wrote **black codes**. Southerners used the black codes to control former slaves, even though slavery was no longer legal.

Because of the black codes, many blacks in the South had to agree to bad labor contracts. The contracts allowed their employers to hold back wages or even beat them. Freedmen needed permission from their employers before they traveled anywhere. They were not allowed to vote.

In this political cartoon, white men take away the rights of former slaves.

The Radical Republicans and other northern politicians worked with the Freedmen's Bureau to correct these wrongs. They wanted the organization to build more schools, homes, and hospitals for blacks in the South. They also wanted the bureau to win better rights for freedmen in their new jobs.

The Freedmen's Bureau was an important agency of the early Reconstruction, assisting freedmen in the South.

NOT SO DIFFERENT FROM SLAVERY

Was life much different for former slaves shortly after the Civil War ended? Freedman Henry Adams didn't think so. In 1865, he reported, "I saw white men whipping colored men just the same as they did before the war." An official with the Freedmen's Bureau agreed and observed that "Blacks are frequently beaten unmercifully and shot down like wild beasts."

Southern black codes forced former slaves to agree to unfair labor contracts.

In February 1866, Congress tried to extend the life of the Freedmen's Bureau, but Johnson vetoed the bill. The president did not believe the U.S. government should tell former Confederate states how to treat the freedmen. He did not think improving the lives of blacks was important.

Radical Republicans passed a series of progressive laws and amendments in Congress that protected blacks' rights under federal and constitutional law.

Congress would not accept Johnson's decision and wrote a second bill in March addressing civil rights. The Civil Rights Act granted citizenship to all males in the United States, regardless of their skin color. Up to that point, former slaves were not considered U.S. citizens. The act also guaranteed black men the same basic rights as white men. Johnson tried to stop this bill as well. He argued that giving blacks equal rights harmed white people. However, Congress was determined. Enough members of Congress voted yes to overrule the president's veto. Johnson could not stop the bill. The Civil Rights Act became law on April 9, 1866.

The struggle between Johnson and the Radical Republicans did not end there. Northern politicians, such as Thaddeus Stevens, had their own plans for Reconstruction. They did not want to return to the way things were before the war. They believed that Reconstruction was a chance to build a new nation. They wanted blacks to enjoy the same opportunities as whites.

Thaddeus Stevens, a Radical Republican, wanted to protect the rights of freedmen.

Thaddeus Stevens (1792–1868)

> "Every negro is required to be in the regular service of some white person, or former owner, who shall be held responsible for his or her conduct... But this employer or former owner may permit the negro to hire his own time by granting him or her special permission in writing."
> —Louisiana black code

Congress passed the Fourteenth Amendment to the U.S. Constitution in July 1866. The change to the Constitution made the ideas of the Civil Rights Act permanent. It reinforced the idea that former slaves were now U.S. citizens. The amendment also tried to protect black men's right to vote in national elections. It said that the country's laws should apply equally to blacks and whites.

Stevens and other Radical Republicans wanted to be sure that white southerners could not rob former slaves of their freedoms. Still, these men also understood that more laws were needed to give blacks true equality. They continued to override Johnson's vetoes to set their plan into action.

> "I have chosen this that I might illustrate in my death the principles which I advocated through a long life: the equality of man before his creator."
> —Tombstone of Thaddeus Stevens, Radical Republican

Chapter 4

STRONGER CHANGE TO COME

With enough votes to override the president, the Radical Republicans in Congress took charge. Congress passed a series of laws that took power away from the southern states.

The state governments that formed under Johnson were broken apart. The majority of southern states, including Texas, Arkansas, Louisiana, Mississippi, Alabama, Georgia, Florida, South Carolina, North Carolina, and Virginia were divided into military districts. These areas would not be controlled by former Confederates but by Republican governors instead.

Congress also called for new state elections. However, former Confederate officials were not allowed to run for office. In addition, new laws protected freedmen's right to vote. Whites would no longer be allowed to frighten or physically harm black voters. Union soldiers would stand guard as African-Americans went to vote. For a short time starting in 1867, black men throughout the South voted in large numbers. They cast their votes for Republicans, those members of Lincoln's party. Republicans took control of state governments throughout the South.

At first, the South seemed destined for great changes. Schools opened across the region for both whites and blacks. Black men also became members of state legislatures for the first time.

Across the South, schools opened to educate freedmen.

CARPETBAGGERS

How did carpetbaggers earn their nickname? The northern travelers often arrived in the South carrying carpetbags, or traveling sacks made from carpet scraps. Southerners believed these businessmen took advantage of the war-torn region by taking whatever treasures and financial opportunities they could find for themselves.

The South's economy also improved. Ambitious businessmen from the North called **carpetbaggers** saw opportunities in the changing South. They flooded the region and started setting up farms and factories. Poor people's taxes were lowered. People were no longer put in jail for having debts.

This cartoon shows the negative attitude some people had toward carpetbaggers.

Freedmen who could not afford land of their own often became sharecroppers.

Senator Charles Sumner believed that Reconstruction was failing to truly help freedmen. He wanted to give plantations that were owned by wealthy southerners to poor whites and blacks. Ultimately, this idea never took off in Congress. While many northerners wanted to help the freedmen, they thought taking away people's land and giving it to others was too severe a punishment, even for treasonous southerners.

STANDING UP FOR FORMER SLAVES

When Senator Sumner suggested that plantations be redistributed among freedmen, one congressman replied, "This is more than we do for white men." Sumner was dedicated to aiding former slaves in the South, especially after they had spent so many years in chains. He responded, "White men have never been in slavery."

Congress's changes upset many white southerners. They felt as if their way of life had been turned upside down. Johnson sympathized with these people. But he could do little to stop the changes.

Meanwhile, Congress carried on. It ordered each former Confederate state to create a new constitution. Each state had to approve the Fourteenth Amendment, which said that former slaves were citizens. Each state also had to promise to protect everyone's right to vote. By 1868 Arkansas, Alabama, Florida, Louisiana, North Carolina, South Carolina, and Tennessee all met these requirements.

Unfortunately, Reconstruction did not solve all of the freedmen's problems. Unable to afford land of their own, many freedmen turned to **sharecropping**. They rented pieces of plantation owners' property. They paid rent with a portion of their crops. If the harvest was bad, sharecroppers easily slipped into debt.

But the freedmen faced even greater problems from the Ku Klux Klan (KKK). This hate group was made up of angry, white southerners who felt that white people should control black people. Members of the KKK often wore white robes with hoods that covered their faces while they carried out their attacks. The robes hid the Klansmen's identities. The robes also frightened the KKK's victims. KKK members hoped they would look like the ghosts of Confederate soldiers who died during the Civil War.

Members of the Ku Klux Klan were bitter about the freedoms Radical Republicans had granted to former slaves. Klansmen targeted freedmen, Union troops, and local officials who were appointed by Radical Republicans. Sometimes they set fire to their victims' homes and businesses. On other occasions, they beat their victims or murdered them by hanging them from trees.

While conflict spread across the South, tension was also growing in Washington, D.C. In 1868, Radical Republicans tried to remove Johnson from office. However, their effort failed by one vote. By November of that year, it was time to elect a new national leader. The nation waited eagerly to see who would win the presidency. Everyone wondered how the new president would manage Reconstruction and the changing South.

GETTING RID OF THE PRESIDENT

Why did Congress try to remove Johnson from office? Some Congress members said the president removed the secretary of war from office in August 1867 without their permission. According to the law, the president was supposed to ask Congress before firing any Cabinet official. The Radical Republicans had argued with Johnson since he took office. They jumped at the chance to destroy his political power.

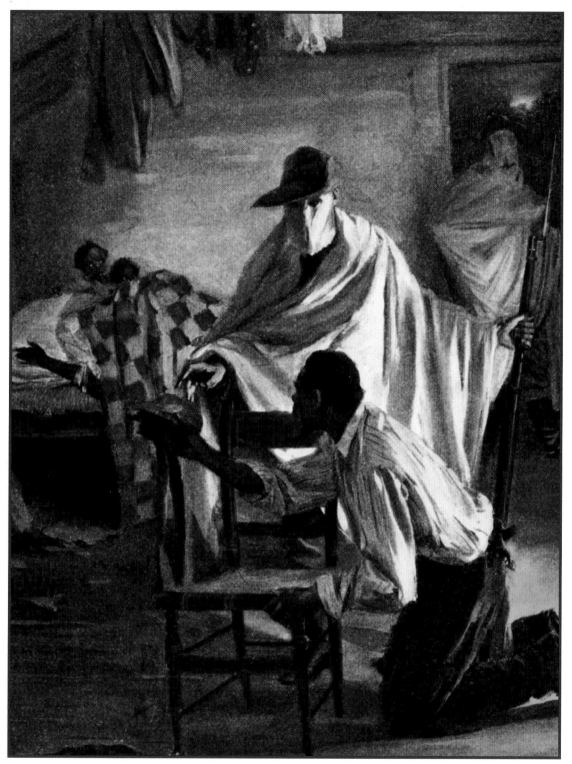

The Ku Klux Klan was one of a number of secret, oath-bound organizations using violence against blacks as intimidation.

The Ku Klux Klan and other white southerners made life for black people almost as difficult as slavery, as shown in this famous cartoon.

Chapter 5
AN ERA OF CHANGE

Republicans wanted a leader who would support their Reconstruction plan. They hoped former Union general and Civil War hero Ulysses S. Grant would help them. He won the 1868 election and was sworn into office on March 4, 1869.

However, Grant was unable to make the Republicans' plan more popular across the country. White southern Democrats were taking back power. These so-called Redeemers began to take back control, or redeem their governments.

As the KKK caused unrest, white southerners pushed for a return to their old way of life. They hated the taxes they paid for Reconstruction programs that aided former slaves. They did not want blacks to have equal rights. Meanwhile, freedmen battled for even basic rights.

Radical Republicans had hoped that the Fourteenth Amendment would guarantee black men the right to vote. Yet many other people refused to admit that it protected that right. Congress decided to make its support of black voting rights even clearer. The result was the Fifteenth Amendment, which was added to the U.S. Constitution on February 3, 1870. The amendment guaranteed the voting rights of black men whether they had once been slaves or not. The first black man took office in the U.S. Congress in 1870.

The southern states now had to accept the new amendment. In July 1870, Georgia was the last state to accept the Fifteenth Amendment. This made Georgia the final Confederate state to rejoin the Union. Was Reconstruction finally at an end?

Many southerners believed the answer was no. While most federal troops departed from the South, not all of the soldiers were gone. Many white southerners did not agree with the rights the U.S. government gave blacks. Freedmen still suffered violence from Klansmen and other whites.

At the same time, the country's attention began to turn away from issues of the Reconstruction. Congress and the Radical Republicans were no longer as quick to aid the freedmen as they had been right after the war. After nearly a decade, northerners' attention turned to western settlements and new economic problems.

LASTING HATRED

The U.S. government tried to end the Ku Klux Klan in the 1870s. However, officials never could get rid of the group. Even today, the KKK uses violence and destroys property to express its members' hatred for other races and religions. Americans have come a long way since Reconstruction. Today, citizens and government officials work together to protect the rights of people from all backgrounds.

Ulysses S. Grant (1822–1885)

Ulysses S. Grant, the leader of the Union army at the end of the Civil War, was president of the United States when the Fifteenth Amendment passed.

Radical Republican Charles Sumner wanted to take away plantations from rebellious southerners and give them to freedmen.

Charles Sumner (1811–1874)

Yet the issue of Reconstruction was not dead. By the presidential election of 1876, it still played a major role. Republican Rutherford B. Hayes ran against Democrat Samuel Tilden. The election was complicated, and the winner was unclear. In the end, Hayes became president, but not before he and the Republicans had to agree to certain conditions by the Democrats. All federal troops in the South had to leave. Hayes had to promise that he would grant southern Democrats larger roles in national politics. All southern state governments were allowed to fall under the control of the Democrats. The future president approved these terms. Reconstruction was over in March 1877.

UNEQUAL LAWS

From the late 1870s to the mid-1960s, southerners who believed in separate rights for separate races passed what were known as Jim Crow laws. These local and state rules denied blacks equality in education and other day-to-day activities. People of other racial backgrounds were often not allowed to attend school or even share public places with whites. The laws were not overturned until the civil rights movement in the mid-twentieth century.

Rutherford B. Hayes (1822–1893)

President Rutherford B. Hayes removed the last federal troops from the South.

After Reconstruction ended, Ku Klux Klan members still spread terror throughout the South.

Eventually, Redeemers took full control of the South. They cut taxes that aided the freedmen. Local laws and customs continued to deny rights to nonwhites. For many years, black people did not have equality in jobs or education. The special government programs to help them escape poverty and racial hatred were over.

The South would not remain this way forever. By the mid-twentieth century, people of all races in every part of the country united to fight for equality and freedom. This time is known as the civil rights movement.

Reconstruction was only the beginning of efforts to rebuild the United States and create a better society after a long and painful war.

"The trials and sufferings of this race have been great for centuries. They have not yet ceased. They are not likely to cease for a long time to come. It may take two or three generations for the race to get a firm and assured status in the land."
—Reverend Alexander Crummell, black leader, 1895

BIOGRAPHIES

Many people played important roles throughout this time period. Learn more about them in the Biographies section.

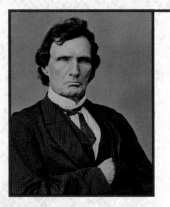

Stevens, Thaddeus (1792–1868) - Stevens was a Radical Republican congressman who served in the House of Representatives during the Civil War and Reconstruction eras. He was deeply against slavery before the war. He was determined to help the freedmen rebuild their lives and win as many rights as possible.

Johnson, Andrew (1808–1875) - Johnson was the seventeenth president of the United States and took office after Lincoln died in April 1865. Johnson had a tense, unhappy relationship with the Senate and the House of Representatives during most of his term. Congress tried to remove him from office in 1868 but failed to do so.

Lincoln, Abraham (1809–1865) - Lincoln was the sixteenth president of the United States. He served from 1861 to 1865, during the Civil War. A quiet, honest politician from Illinois, he was openly against slavery. His election prompted several southern states to secede. Lincoln signed the Emancipation Proclamation. He was killed shortly after the Civil War ended in 1865.

Sumner, Charles (1811–1874) - Sumner was a senator who was against slavery before the Civil War and in favor of Radical Reconstruction following it. He supported whatever measures were necessary to help the freedmen. He argued that former slaves and poor whites were entitled to land once held by wealthy southern plantation owners.

Grant, Ulysses S. (1822–1885) - Grant was the commander of the Union army at the end of the Civil War. He became the eighteenth president of the United States in 1869. Grant served two terms, which ended in 1877. Unfortunately, much of his time in the White House was shaped by government scandal.

Hayes, Rutherford B. (1822–1893) - Hayes won the presidency in 1877 by a slim margin. Reconstruction was the issue that ultimately decided the race. Hayes took office after promising to remove the remaining federal troops from the South. He also granted southern Democrats more political opportunities. His move into the White House marked the official end of Reconstruction.

TIMELINE

January 1, 1863
The Emancipation Proclamation goes into effect.

December 8, 1863
Lincoln issues his plans for Reconstruction.

July 1864
Congress presents its own plan for Reconstruction to Lincoln, who vetoes it.

April 9, 1865
Lee surrenders to Grant in Appomattox Courthouse, essentially ending the Civil War.

April 15, 1865
Lincoln dies after being shot the night before; Johnson is sworn in a few hours later.

Summer 1865
Southern states begin passing black codes.

December 18, 1865
The Thirteenth Amendment is officially added to the U.S. Constitution.

April 9, 1866
The Civil Rights Act is written into law.

March 2, 1867
Congress passes the First Reconstruction Act.

July 9, 1868
The Fourteenth Amendment is officially added to the U.S. Constitution.

March 4, 1869
Grant is sworn into office and becomes the nation's eighteenth president.

February 3, 1870
The Fifteenth Amendment is officially added to the U.S. Constitution.

February 25, 1870
The first African American takes office in the United States Congress.

1876
Various southern states begin to use Jim Crow laws to enforce separate treatment for separate races.

March 4, 1877
Hayes becomes president, and with the Compromise of 1877. Reconstruction is officially considered to be at an end.

REFERENCE

Military Reconstruction

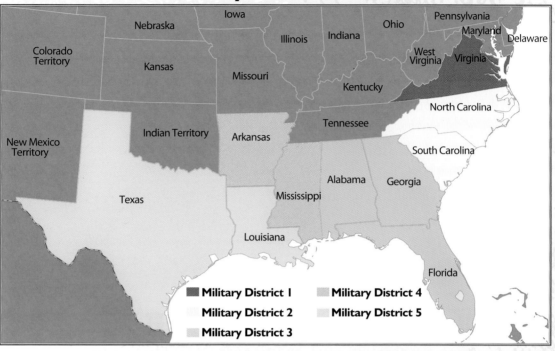

Military District 1
Military District 2
Military District 3
Military District 4
Military District 5

1876 Presidential Election

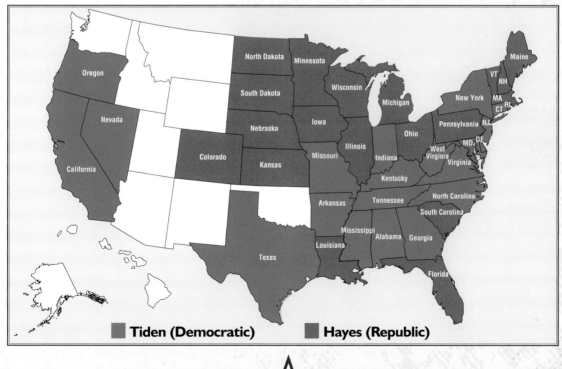

Tiden (Democratic)   Hayes (Republic)

WEBSITES TO VISIT

www.infoplease.com/spot/bhmtimeline.html

chnm.gmu.edu/courses/122/recon/reconframe.html

www.infoplease.com/encyclopedia/history/reconstruction-lincoln-plan.html

SHOW WHAT YOU KNOW

1. Describe Lincoln's Reconstruction plan.

2. Define civil rights.

3. How did southerners use the black codes?

4. What did the Radical Republicans support?

5. What rights did freedmen have during Reconstruction?

GLOSSARY

black codes (BLAK KODES): laws that stripped Southern freedmen of their basic rights

carpetbaggers (KAR-pit-bag-gurz): Northerners who moved to the South in the hopes of building businesses and making their fortunes there during Reconstruction

civil rights (SIV-il RITES): the rights and privileges that all citizens are supposed to share equally

Confederacy (kuhn-FED-ur-uh-see): the states that seceded from the United States; the South

Emancipation Proclamation (i-man-si-PAY-shun prok-la-MAY-shuhn): Lincoln's order that freed slaves in the Confederacy

freedmen (FREED-men): former slaves who have been freed

plantations (plan-TAY-shuhns): large farms that need many workers

seceded (si-SEED-id): left or withdrew from a group

sharecropping (SHAIR-krop-ping): a farming system in which people rent land to farm in exchange for paying the actual landowner a portion of their crops

Union (YOON-yuhn): the states that did not secede from the United States; the North

vetoed (VEE-tohd): stopped a bill from becoming law

INDEX